Facets of Loving

OTHER BOOKS BY JOHN-ROGER, D.S.S.

Blessings of Light
Divine Essence
Dream Voyages
Forgiveness – The Key to the Kingdom
Fulfilling Your Spiritual Promise
God Is Your Partner
Inner Worlds of Meditation
Journey of a Soul
Living Love from the Spiritual Heart
Loving Each Day
Loving Each Day for Moms & Dads
Loving Each Day for Peacemakers
Manual on Using the Light
Passage Into Spirit
The Path to Mastership
The Power Within You
Psychic Protection
Relationships: Love, Marriage & Spirit
Sex, Spirit & You
The Spiritual Family
Spiritual High (with Michael McBay, M.D.)
The Spiritual Promise
Spiritual Warrior: The Art of Spiritual Living
The Tao of Spirit
Timeless Wisdoms, Vol. I
Timeless Wisdoms, Vol. II
Walking With the Lord
The Way Out Book
The Wayshower
Wealth & Higher Consciousness
When Are You Coming Home? (with Pauli Sanderson, D.S.S.)

BOOKS BY JOHN-ROGER, D.S.S., with PAUL KAYE, D.S.S.

Living the Spiritual Principles of Abundance and Prosperity, Vols. 1, 2 & 3
Living the Spiritual Principles of Health and Well-Being
Momentum: Letting Love Lead
Serving & Giving
The Rest of Your Life
What's It Like Being You?

MANDEVILLE PRESS
P.O. Box 513935
Los Angeles, CA 90051-1935
323-737-4055
jrbooks@mandevillepress.org
www.mandevillepress.org

Printed in the United States of America
ISBN: 978-1-936514-71-7

Facets of Loving

John-Roger, D.S.S.
with Betsy Alexander

MANDEVILLE PRESS
Los Angeles, California

Contents

Preface

I sometimes think of John-Roger's consciousness as one of those mirrored balls on the ceiling of a room where people dance. Light shines from each of the ball's many facets, each facet being slightly different.

It seems to me that the Light J-R shines to me is exactly perfect for me and that this is so for everyone he touches. Here are some stories from my memory and my letters and memos of some experiences I've been blessed with from J-R's "Betsy Facet."

Betsy Alexander

April 2013

Meeting J-R

I first heard of the Movement of Spiritual Inner Awareness when I was living in Calexico, then a city of about 10,000 people, east of San Diego on the U.S. side of the Mexican border. One friend there told me a little about MSIA, and I made fun of it, including of John-Roger, a person with just one name, and one with a hyphen to boot. My friend was indulgent of my skepticism.

After separating from my husband, I began exploring spirituality, starting with *Be Here Now* by Ram Dass and Zen Buddhism. I tried to meditate, not very successfully. One time as I was trying, I opened my eyes and saw J-R standing in front of me, slightly to my right. I hadn't met him, but I knew it was J-R. I shut and opened my eyes: still there.

That summer (1973), I started having numbness in my feet. I was very worried, thinking I would die a slow and—even more important—expensive death. Lying in bed one night, worrying, I remembered that Ram Dass had written,"The guru is within you." I thought, "John-Roger," and immediately was filled with peace and went into a deep sleep. I called MSIA and ordered Discourses the next day. The numbness faded away, as did any concern about that hyphenated name.

I've often thought that if J-R could find me in Calexico, he could find anyone anywhere. Much later I discovered that he had said, "This path of Soul Transcendence is not for everyone at this time. It is for those who had it 'written on their foreheads' before the foundation of the planet that this would be their time."

I first met J-R physically at the 1974 MSIA Conference held in June at the San Gabriel Civic Auditorium. In those days, Conference was just one day: a morning session and an afternoon session with a lunch break during which people could buy food in the courtyard outside. As my Calexico friend and I wandered in the courtyard during the break, we ran into J-R, walking by himself. My friend introduced us and we shook hands. I said, "I'm glad to be here," and he replied, "We're glad you're here." Both of us were wearing sunglasses, but I could see his eyes clearly. After he left, I said something to my friend that I didn't understand then: "It was like shaking hands with Jesus."

In a letter I wrote to J-R about 30 years later, I was musing about what the disciple Peter said (in response to Jesus' asking him, "You do not want to leave too, do you?"). In my letter, I quoted Peter's reply to Jesus: "To whom shall we go? You have the words of eternal life." J-R wrote, "With me." I think that applies to everyone doing Soul Transcendence with J-R.

Working on MSIA Staff

When I took Insight II right before the 1979 MSIA Conference, I realized that what I really wanted was to join the MSIA staff. At Conference, I ambushed J-R as he was walking in the hallway of the Sheraton Universal Hotel: "Can I talk to you?"

"How long will it take?"

"Thirty seconds."

"Okay."

"I want to be on MSIA staff."

After a pause, "Talk to Pauli." This was Pauli McGarry (now Sanderson), the MSIA administrator.

I wrote Pauli at the office, and she replied in a very kind letter, explaining how being on staff worked then (most living at Prana, etc.). It took me five years, but it happened in 1984, and I also realized that being on staff is a training in itself.

Loving

Someone recently asked me what J-R's leadership style is from my personal experience, and I listed these qualities: loving, honesty, clarity, vision, and delegating/empowering. Then, as I was working on this book, I realized that freedom is another hallmark of his approach. I'll start with loving, which I think is fundamental to everything he does and is.

J-R has said, "I love because *I* love." I understand that to mean that the love is within him and is not dependent on anything or anyone outside himself.

For example, there was a legal situation during which J-R gave a deposition over several days; he asked if I'd like to attend one session, so I went.

As we were leaving, the person who brought the legal action ended up in the elevator with J-R and those of us supporting him. J-R gave the person a big hug, and I saw the loving in his eyes. I don't think J-R holds anyone as an enemy inside himself, but for me this was a breath-taking example of what Jesus said: "Love your enemies, do good to those who would harm you."

J-R also wrote in the early nineties, "When it comes to spiritual things, we are all always on the cutting edge. It seems as though I have never been off of it. Consequently I have gotten quite used to it. That doesn't make it easier in any way, shape, or form. It is that I am familiar with the 'negative' feelings that can go with this type of work. I also know that we can clear all of them with love, Light, and laughter."

One person asked J-R if a woman, who was well-known for devoting herself to helping the poor, would go to the Soul realm when she died and not need to incarnate again. J-R said no, explaining to the effect that she loved only *poor* people.

J-R asked me one evening about an MSIA building project. After I gave him the update, he told me there was "no rush on it. We just do the best we can with loving. And if we die along the way, we go to heaven."

One time, maybe 25 or so years ago, I was very upset about an ongoing situation. J-R called and told me to leave the office, go out to dinner, and see a movie. He also said, "If anyone asks you what you are doing, say you're doing an errand for J-R." I was gone within 15 minutes. His caring meant much more to me than whatever I ate and whatever movie I saw.

At one MSIA event, some of us were sitting around chatting. J-R sat with his arm around one woman, and at first, I was a little envious of their physical closeness. But as I continued to observe, I realized—and felt—that his love wasn't exclusive, just for her, but was for all of us, as if he had his arm around each one of us.

J-R is the most loving person I've ever known, and there are more stories about this in the rest of the book. And I think this sums it up: when I ended one work email to J-R with "I love you," he wrote back, "Thank you. Love is how this all works."

Freedom

J-R is also the freest person I've ever known, an integral part, I think, of being loving in the highest sense. He has said, "The Traveler is freedom, expresses freedom, and gives freedom." My personality often wants orderliness and efficiency, which can sometimes get in the way of loving and freedom and which can also slide into bureaucracy. Here are some stories that helped me understand that J-R and MSIA don't run on rules.

When J-R and some staff first went to Nigeria in the mid-eighties, J-R approved the causal initiation for a man who was not taking Discourses, and the initiation was done. Subsequently, the man never got Discourses and never even got in touch with us.

One summer, all the staffs of the organizations J-R founded had a retreat at the MSIA property at Lake Arrowhead. One evening, we watched a slide show of a recent PAT IV trip to Egypt and Israel. There was one stunning photo of a smiling girl who looked about 15 years old. As I recall, she was standing behind a wrought-iron fence or gate; she looked radiant. In questions afterwards, my memory is that J-R said they were walking in Egypt and he heard Spirit tell him things like, "Turn right here, go straight, turn left," etc. He got to this girl behind the fence and initiated her—no initiation tones given, just his looking at her. One person in the Arrowhead group asked if she got her causal initiation. J-R said, "She got her Soul initiation."

In the mid-seventies, Vincent Dupont asked J-R why MSIA has no rules for doing Soul Transcendence, as other groups have for what they teach (for example, how to dress, what to eat, etc.). J-R said it's because he holds the 27 keys of fulfillment, which correspond to the 27 levels above Soul. Other people in other groups need the discipline or experience those groups provide.

J-R told me once that "if people don't read their Discourses, they can reincarnate and pick it up again. We don't interfere." He has also said, "I do not enter into your physical life or tell you what to do or what not to do; that's for you to decide." To me, this shows deep respect for each person and an honoring of their choices, and in this respect and honoring, there is enormous freedom. I love that this attitude is foundational to the work we do at MSIA.

In November 1974, I met with J-R for a Light Study. Before I saw him, a staff member filled out a form that included a question about drug use, and I said I had used marijuana and LSD. When I walked into the room where we would talk, J-R was looking at the form. Even before we sat down, he asked, "Are you going for initiation?" Yes. "No more drugs." That was it for me. And he was never judgmental or admonishing. I realized later that this was a great example of how J-R gives the information and then we choose what we do. As he has said, "You are, as always, free to 'take it or leave it.'"

J-R has told us on staff that our mission "is to make the teachings of the Traveler available to those who are looking for them." And he has also said, "This Movement is for those people who find it, and we do not proselytize. If people find us, fine. If not, equally fine. We do not focus on how many people are studying in the Church, and it is not required that MSIA participants bring in new people, but they may do that just by living the teachings." I love the freedom in this.

Someone was concerned about the Light not being called in formally at an event hosted by one of MSIA's sister organizations. J-R wrote, "I could not believe that anyone in their right mind has to believe that the Light can only be called in vocally. Each person can call it in by just thinking about it. Of course, if they are into ritual, then they would not think that the Light came into the group unless the ritual was done. Poppycock." And, of course, it's fine for people to call in the Light and chant Hu or Ani-Hu as a group.

Once when I was talking with J-R about a book, he said he wanted to emphasize a word, so it should be in CAPS. From my background in academic copyediting, I said, "To emphasize something, we put it in *italic.*" He said, "Put it in **bold,** too." Needless to say, I dropped it there, thinking—probably correctly—that if I continued, he'd say to put it in ***BOLD ITALIC CAPS.*** It was another example of his teaching me about not being a slave to rules.

As a sidenote, J-R had asked me to come to his home to discuss that book, which I think was the first time I had gone there to meet with him individually. In addition to being excited as I drove there, I was nervous because, at that time, J-R had two Rottweilers—large dogs with very loud barks and very big jaws. But when I walked into the kitchen, the dogs were deeply asleep on the floor and didn't move a paw while I was there. I'm guessing that J-R picked up on my trepidation and told or asked the dogs to go to sleep.

J-R is also free—and unpredictable—in what he says. One of my favorite examples of this was when a good friend of mine came to a seminar he gave at Prana, something I had been secretly wanting her to do for years. She is gay, and I really hoped that J-R would be his best nonsexist self during the seminar.

Before the seminar started, I introduced my friend to J-R in the back of the room. She surprised me by saying that she had once been on the same flight to Mexico that he was on. It came out that she had been traveling with her husband, and she told him they were now divorced.

J-R asked her, "What's a good-looking woman like you doing without a husband?" I started to get nervous.

She asked, "What should a woman look for in a man?"

"Money." Now I was really nervous and went on the offensive: "Well, what should a man look for in a woman?"

With a quick glance and a small grin at me, he said to her, complete with hand motions, "Big tits."

I was vanquished. My friend and I sat down, and she very mildly said, "He sure knows how to push people's buttons." That made me feel a little better. I felt much better when I realized that J-R probably couldn't say anything in the seminar "worse" than what he had told her, so I relaxed and enjoyed the evening. I also got a lesson about not trying to manipulate him into saying or doing what I wanted.

Another lesson I got about not messing with J-R happened during a staff Christmas party at a restaurant. After arriving, I put my purse and jacket on a chair and went into the restroom. When I returned, I was surprised to find J-R sitting to my left. During dinner, we were chatting about the Integrity Foundation award to Bishop Desmond Tutu. J-R seemed not to remember who Bishop Tutu was, and I cheekily said, "You know, he's the short guy with curly hair." He looked at me and said quietly, "I'll get you."

Later during dinner, I was talking to someone across from me when my mind suddenly stopped working and I had no words for a few moments. Then the only thing I could say was, "Rats." He grinned at me and said, "I told you I'd get you." It was pretty funny to all of us at the table—and I never did figure out how he did that.

As a second sidenote, later that evening one staff member who lived at Prana said he wanted to get a dog. I was glad to hear J-R say, "No dogs at Prana."

Honesty

One time I was trying to explain to J-R how I felt about a situation. I remember saying, "J-R, I'm trying to be honest about this." His reply: "You wouldn't know the truth if it came up and kissed you on the forehead." I was shocked and speechless. It took me about a year to get to what I think he was telling me: I didn't want to know the truth about what was really going on for me because I was too self-judgmental.

Another time I was upset by the actions of a staff member with whom I had to work. J-R called me with some questions that evening. At the end, he asked me how I was. When I said I was okay, he asked, "How *are* you?"

I figured he really did want to know—or, actually, already knew and was giving me a chance to tell him so he could assist. So I told him about the interaction with the staff member. J-R said I should tell that person about it, and I said, "But, J-R, I'll cry."

He told me, "That person needs to know how upset you are."

I did talk to the person, I did cry, and that person changed. It was another reminder to be honest and not slide over something.

One evening, I told J-R about someone's having viral meningitis, a painful and debilitating illness. He said something like, "That's really hard." And after a pause, he added, "But it will end." I loved that he was honest about this person's very difficult situation and that he then gave words of hope.

Years ago, Paul Kaye wrote to J-R at the end of a series of emails from a number of people about a situation Paul had brought up: "I am sorry to have created a fuss. I should have kept my mouth shut, or at least my keyboard." J-R replied, "Not so. Open communication is the lifeblood of these organizations."

I once tried to find a letter J-R wanted. After scouring my files, I told him I couldn't find it. He was noncommittal. A day or so later, I realized I hadn't checked the files kept off-site. I did and found it. When I called to tell him and apologize, he said to the effect that it was no problem—but it would have been a problem if I *hadn't* told him. Honesty, no withholds.

Clarity

One of the things we on staff are trained to do is follow up in writing when decisions are made. J-R wrote it this way on one memo: "We have a long-standing policy that all verbal agreements of any kind have to be followed up with a written confirmation, or the verbal agreements just don't count."

We've also been encouraged to have our communications be clear, clean, and concise. I had a great experience of this years ago, before email. There were times when J-R and some staff would travel to various parts of the U.S., sometimes being gone for three months at a time. We'd over-night paper memos to him, and he would sometimes give feedback on the phone through one of the staff with him. J-R would say a phrase, and the staff member would repeat it to me; this continued until J-R's entire comments were communicated.

One evening I got a call from John Morton, saying J-R wanted clarification about something I had sent to him. I saw how what I had written could be misinterpreted and explained what I meant. John told J-R and then gave me J-R's reply, in phrases:

"J-R says . . .

"if you can't give clear information . . .

"just shut the f--- up."

When we ended the call soon after that, I burst out laughing and was elated. I had arrived. J-R had treated me like one of his staff guys.

Vision

When J-R received the keys to the Mystical Traveler Consciousness (December 3 to 23, 1963), I don't know if he saw ahead to the organizations that formed around him over the following years, and I have heard him say several times that he never wanted an organization, since organizations can become "beasts." In fact, MSIA was not incorporated as a church until January 1971.

J-R has also said, "The Movement of Spiritual Inner Awareness (MSIA) is not necessary to the Traveler's work of Soul Transcendence. It is a church structure for legal purposes." He added that "the Traveler is currently using MSIA as a vehicle to support its work on the physical level." This, to me, is another wonderful example of J-R's freedom.

And since I work for MSIA, I am rather attached to it. I once said that to J-R and, I think, thanked him for looking out for MSIA. He told me that "MSIA is my 'baby,' and I don't kill babies." I have also seen him repeatedly guide and correct how MSIA functions organizationally and how we on staff work within it.

For example, one staff person wanted to institute procedures that moved away from MSIA's approach of just giving the information and then letting people make their own choices. J-R said that the proposed changes wouldn't be put in place because the person's "point of view is correct on the physical ego level, but not on the spiritual level." I'm deeply grateful to work for and be involved in an organization that, through J-R, is truly Spirit-directed.

I think J-R's vision is multidimensional, and he once told me, "Seeing is above all." I have my inner experiences of that and have also had some on this level. For example, we were doing work on the phone one evening, and in the middle of it, he said, "An earthquake's coming." About 10 seconds later, I felt a small earthquake. I asked how he knew, and he said he had seen it.

I have also heard stories about how J-R laid out the trails at the Lake Arrowhead property so they wouldn't encroach on the areas where there are devas, which he apparently could see.

This one may not exactly be in the "seeing" category, but I like it a lot. I once saw a man ask J-R to bless a wedding ring (it could have been two rings). J-R held the ring and said, "It has already been blessed by a Traveler." The man said no and that it had recently been made to order. J-R repeated what he had said. The man then realized that the metal in the ring came at least partly from his previous wedding ring, which had been melted down and used in the new ring. And J-R had, in fact, blessed that previous ring.

After an event at Prana a couple of years ago, J-R called me over and said, "We should write a book together." I sort of shined him on because I liked editing and copyediting books by him, but I didn't want to be a "co-author." Still, I never discounted what he said since I figured he was probably envisioning something I couldn't yet see. During the 2012 MSIA Conference, I started getting ideas for how to do a book with him, and then I got into the great fun and joy of remembering stories and looking through my memos and letters.

I also highly recommend Pauli McGarry Sanderson's stories about J-R, the beginnings of MSIA, and its growth. It's in *Fulfilling Your Spiritual Promise* and is called "An Informal History of MSIA." I think it wonderfully captures the spirit, energy, and fun of those times.

On a more personal note, there was an MSIA event that included a boat ride in San Diego. During this time, I was going through difficulties and felt sad. On the boat, J-R and I ended up standing together by the rail, looking out over the ocean. He pointed out how the sunlight was sparkling on the water and said that "this is what Souls look like before they incarnate." That lifted my sights from my immediate situation and reminded me of the larger picture, the greater vision.

I think J-R holds this greater vision for all of us, seeing us as who we really are, as Souls. So even when we are in our karma, he goes through it with us while still knowing the spiritual truth about us.

Delegating/Empowering

J-R is my favorite kind of boss, the opposite of a micromanager, letting me run with various projects after he's approved them and being available when I have questions. And he's lived up to what he told me in the mid-seventies during a retreat at Lake Arrowhead. I was working with a group to put segments of telephone poles on the incline of a hill, to make a sort of amphitheater. I was annoyed that the leader of the group was not being as efficient as I thought she should be. J-R strolled by and asked how I was doing. I probably said I was okay. He said, "You know, there's more than one right way to do something."

J-R's encouragement has let my creativity soar. I've made plenty of mistakes and, I hope, learned from them. When I've done a good job, I've felt deep satisfaction that I could help him and do something useful. He might have done things differently, but there's more than one right way to do something. Also, had he not—from the very beginning of his work—delegated to staff and others, none of us would have had the chance to share the joy and blessings of doing this work. As he says, part of what he teaches is "loving, caring, and *sharing.*"

J-R has also said that "the willingness to do gives the ability to do, and the reward for doing is the ability to do more." This seemed depressing to me when I was extremely busy. Then I realized that he kept giving me chances to do, to expand both inwardly and outwardly, which allowed me to have the fun and fulfillment of that.

Although J-R is not a micromanager, he's quite precise when it's called for. For example, when he was at Prana once, I walked with him as he was showing someone around. In the products department, he saw the new edition of the Discourses and picked up Discourse 1. Holding the Discourse to one side of his face but looking straight at me, he quickly ruffled through it and said, "No typos." Whew. I had proofed it.

There is also the time I sent J-R a letter from someone, and he kept asking gentle questions about it. I finally backtracked and found that I had given him the wrong name for the person. When I told him, he said he knew the name had been wrong. Then he said something that went much deeper than any chewing-out would have: "I count on you to give me accurate information." How amazing to hear that he counted on me. This made me want to become even more trustworthy and was another way he has empowered me.

Some More Staff Stories

Over the years, I have sometimes given my point of view on various situations at work and at Prana, and when J-R agreed with me, I was glad to know I was on track. I'm not saying he always agreed with me. For example, I wrote one memo, laying out how I saw something and what we should do. J-R said no and also clearly explained why. Then he wrote, "I love you and your ability to think independently from the so-called 'party policy.'"

I see that approach in two things I've heard him say a number of times throughout the years. The first is to "ask the 'dumb' questions" in order to understand a situation. The second is to "be intellectually honest" and look at both (all) sides of any question or situation. In my experience over the years, J-R has had no problem at all hearing differing ideas and points of view. In fact, he has welcomed them.

Once when we were doing some work on the phone, I mentioned to J-R, probably with a little weariness in my voice, that I was "caught up on letters—for now." He said that there are lots of dishes to wash after a big family meal, and that means everyone was well-fed. What a wonderful reframe.

There was a time when we were having a lot of problems with our computer system and the copiers. I told J-R about this, asking for Light, and he made suggestions along these lines: go to each computer and copier in the building and bless it and put Light into it. A group of us did this, and my recall is that the problems stopped.

J-R was asked about burning epsom salts and rubbing alcohol to clear the room during breaks in an event. He replied, "It is paganism. And, also, if you light the alcohol on fire, you must be careful about the alcoholic entities since they enjoy that sort of thing." Instead, J-R recommended that the assistants and facilitators call in the Light during breaks to clear the room.

Early in my staff career, I was trying to do work with him on the phone, but he had his phone on speaker mode, and it was very hard for me to hear him. We ended the call, and I remember saying to another staff member, with some energy, "If he wants to talk to me, he has to *pick up the phone!*" Within 10 minutes, he called me back—no speaker phone this time. Looks like he heard me.

And speaking of phones, one Christmas Day, I cleared the answer machine and found a message from J-R. I called him back and said something like, "It's Christmas and you're working." He said, "I'm always working."

Take Care of Yourself

One of the MSIA guidelines is to "take care of yourself so you can help take care of others." J-R says that how we take care of ourselves is our responsibility, and he doesn't tell people what to do or interfere with their choices. To me, that's part of the freedom J-R brings to everything he does. And to glimpse this from his side, a person once wrote to J-R with thanks "for all your patience and for your willingness to let us learn what we must learn." J-R's answer: "This has been my greatest struggle in the physical plane." And here are a couple of experiences that had an impact on me.

Once when I was in a super-busy period, J-R called the office around midnight. I answered the phone, and he asked me why I was working so late. With a tinge of self-pity, I said, "There's so much work to do." He told me that if I run out of work to do, I won't have a job. He also said something about taking care of myself "or it could turn into resentment."

Another time I was concerned that a fellow staff person was getting really tired and, in my mind, was overworked. I mentioned this to J-R in an email, my hidden agenda being that I wanted J-R to intervene and change things. J-R's response: "I guess the person likes it." Another reminder to me that we are responsible for our choices and for taking care of ourselves.

Perfection

A woman on staff sent a cross to J-R to bless. Months later, it hadn't come back from him via our interoffice mail, and I'd periodically feel concerned and wonder why. This woman was very close to a woman who was like her mother. The older woman died, and the staff member was grieving. The day she returned to work, her blessed cross came back from J-R. Perfect timing.

J-R once wrote to a manager, "I don't want it run perfectly, otherwise the team won't be able to work off any karma. However, you can tell them where you see their physical performance being less than on course."

At one time, I was annoyed with a woman who kept telling me about all the important things she did, the famous people she knew, and so on. I mentioned this to J-R, and he said—in the most neutral voice possible—"She's always promoting herself." His neutrality took the wind out of my sails. It was another example of his simply describing what was going on, without judgment, and not making her or me wrong. It also reminded me of what he says: "The world is perfect. You just don't like it that way."

J-R encouraged me to apply that view of "perfect" to myself when I once wrote him a rather theoretical letter about learning to change myself. His spot-on response: "Learning is seen in the change in behavior, not in verbalized mental thoughts." He added at the end, "Give yourself a break, and don't put this in the 'be perfect' category. If we are going to do any of this work, let's have as much fun as possible."

J-R has also put it this way: "Even though the things we do in this physical world may continually misrepresent who we are, let's never forget for even one second that the divine spark that is God resides within each one of us. And after all has been said and done, you'll find out that you've been walking with your own Beloved for many, many eons. And one of your great realizations will be that, at all times, everything was absolutely perfect within you."

Books

In the late seventies, I was living in Fresno, California, and had decided to quit my job and move to Pasadena, to be closer to MSIA activities. Before I moved, I dreamed that J-R hugged me and asked, "Do you want to get married or write a book about MSIA—work for me?" I said, "Work for you."

I joined the MSIA staff in 1984 and kept looking for that book he told me about in the dream. In 1991, I started thinking about what became *Fulfilling Your Spiritual Promise,* which was done in late 2006. A while before its publication, I apologetically mentioned to J-R that it was taking so many years to complete it, and he said something like he knew it would take someone with "perseverance and patience" to do it. That relieved me.

J-R is masterful at editing. For example, when I was compiling *Fulfilling Your Spiritual Promise,* there was this sentence in one chapter: "Judgment evicts the Christ." As usual for each of his books, I sent that chapter to him to review. When he returned it, I saw that he had edited that sentence to read like this: "Judgment tries to evict the Christ." Another time he changed "the Traveler is the heart of the universe" to "the Traveler is the heart of all the universes."

And J-R is clear that Spirit does the work. He once edited an article someone wrote for an MSIA newsletter, cutting the last paragraph, which was about him, and giving this feedback: "Best not to nudge people to the [my] physical form when it is the spiritual form that does the work." Another time, he wrote someone, "When the Spirit hugs people through me, it is more often than not that their lives go through some very nice changes."

"Omit Needless Words"

The Elements of Style by William Strunk Jr. and E.B. White includes this as one of its Elementary Principles of Composition: "Omit needless words." J-R is a master of this and, with just a couple of words, has changed my perspective and my life. Here are some of my favorite stories.

At an MSIA event, J-R introduced a technique that we could use for spiritual protection. As I recall, he said to the effect that our using this technique would make things harder on the Travelers. Concerned, I asked what we could do to make things easier. His response: "Be nice." I'm still working on that.

A person living at Prana wrote to J-R about the removal of several trees from the orchard, saying something like they felt sad every time they looked at where the trees used to be. J-R's response was, "Stop looking." I've applied that since, especially to news coverage.

After I had been on staff 15 years or so, I wrote J-R about feeling guilty that I was not working the number of hours I had when I started, was not doing as much, etc., and I asked for feedback on how I was doing my job. His response: "Be happy."

One time a group of us went to a movie in Santa Monica. As I was driving there, a truck was stopped half in a driveway and half in the street, so I halted about six or seven yards back. Then the truck backed up and kept going even though I honked loudly. The truck crunched the front fender of the car I was driving. The driver got out, said it was entirely his fault, and gave me the phone number of his company. When I called the company about 10 minutes later, I got the boss, who said he had talked to the driver and that it was my fault because the car behind another vehicle is always at fault in an accident like that. I was outraged, but he didn't budge.

When I ran into J-R in the theater lobby, I told him about this, ending with, "J-R, he *lied!*"

J-R said something like, "I've often said, 'People lie.'" That short reminder that "people lie" helped me dial back my anger and frustration, and it also helped that he stood there a while and chatted with me and some others while I simmered down.

Some years back, another staff member and I were sandpapering each other quite a bit as we worked together. I emailed J-R about the situation, copying the other person, and asked for Light and any advice. He wrote back to us both, "Stop being a bitch to each other." It was a bit embarrassing at the time, is funny in retrospect, and was clear direction. It's that "be nice" again.

There was also a time years ago when I had been writing him fairly often about a difficult personal situation I was going through. After several weeks, I ran into him at a Prana event and told him that I was done with the situation, adding, "I'm bored with it." With a grin, he said, "*You're* bored." The man is patient.

The man is also funny. During one staff meeting, I prefaced my question to him by saying, "You're the biggest blessing in my life." His reply:

"If I gained any more weight, I'd be an even bigger blessing." His joke helped me relax.

J-R once co-facilitated an event with another person. A woman there, who had a strong personality, asked a question and got into a verbal tug-of-war with the co-facilitator, who was also quite strong. As it heated up, J-R lay down on his side on the floor, propped his head on his hand, and said, "Fight!" All of us cracked up. The two seemed somewhat hesitant to continue, but J-R urged them on: "Fight! Fight!" As we laughed and applauded, the two seemed to try to argue a bit more and then ran out of steam, ending with a good-natured cease-fire. It was such a great lesson for me about enjoying, rather than being bothered by, people's expression.

At our monthly Prana house meetings, we used to have repeated and seemingly interminable discussions about having cats here, although the guideline is "no pets at Prana." In the early nineties, a staff member wrote up one discussion and sent it to J-R, whose response is one of my all-time favorites: "Your jobs at Prana are not fighting over pussies. But it is Soul Transcendence. If someone tries to lower your sights to pussy, resist it, of course unless that pussy is also doing Soul Transcendence."

About a year later, the subject of cats again came up at a house meeting. A resident wrote to J-R, who responded, "If people at Prana spent as much energy looking into their Soul or finding it, they would be in 'heaven' already. So why get caught up with cats, or any other animal. J-R certainly doesn't." I don't recall any other cat memos after that.

Besides responding succinctly, to the point, and often with humor, J-R is also a master at asking questions. For example, years ago, I disagreed with the actions of a manager on staff. I wrote J-R an email about it, copying the manager. J-R's response to me, which he sent to both of us, was this: "Are you saying you know the karma in the situation?" That brought me to a screeching halt. No, I didn't know the karma. Also, J-R didn't make either me or the manager wrong. Brilliant.

Always with You

One of the things I do on staff is assist J-R with letters people write to him. I have seen time and time again the "magic" that comes with writing to the Traveler—namely, that when someone writes and sends (or burns) their letter, things often start changing for the person. J-R has explained how this works: "I get the letter spiritually when you write it because you and I are in touch through the Mystical Traveler that is in me and that is in you. It is the same Traveler in both of us. The communication is between you and the center of you that is the Traveler."

For example, here's part of a letter from someone to J-R: "After so many years of working with you, I can't say I was too surprised when about 5 minutes after emailing a letter to you, I was able to start coming into balance, both emotionally and physically. Within an hour I was really OK, and by the next day I had my joy back. I don't know why it works, but it's magical—getting to that blatantly honest place that pinpoints the grief and fears, and then releasing it to you. I am so lucky to be alive while you're here on the planet."

J-R addressed this idea in one Question-and-Answer session:

Question: I have so many questions I could ask.

J-R: Why don't you write them on a piece of paper and then sit down and answer them? You have the same ability to tap into the Spirit as I do. But you're lazy, and you won't do it. But you could. You'd end up with almost the same answer. The only real difference is that I've had more experience doing it, and so I probably am going to be able to guess out the answer faster. But once you get the answer, it's going to be the same because the answer is the same when it's true.

Question: You seem so much clearer with your ability to get there and your quickness to get there.

J-R: It's from a lot of practice. That takes nothing away from you. I'm with you all the time. When I'm not there physically, I'm there spiritually. There's no place Travelers are not.

Another person wrote to J-R, "Each time I ask inwardly for your help, it arrives as quickly as the prayer is made. It is a daily prayer, sometimes many times a day, as I call forward my inner Traveler and ask for assistance. I know that each time I ask for help, it is present." J-R also gets the information spiritually as soon as someone puts a name on any of the MSIA Prayer Lists or when someone leaves a message at the MSIA office or The Heartfelt Foundation office.

Question: If I ask inwardly for you to send the Light to someone, is that less effective than if I talk or write to you or call the MSIA office and ask that you do this?

J-R: It's just as effective to ask inwardly. You can also write to me and burn the letter. It doesn't have to be done physically because the work I do is done spiritually, and it's done instantly, as soon as you ask inwardly.

One of my favorite J-R responses was on an email to a staff person who had used our walkie-talkie system earlier in the day to tell him about a problem. She wrote to him, "Thanks for being available for us today. It is such a blessing knowing you are just a walkie call away." J-R's reply: "I am much closer than that. Really."

That's a spiritual promise I hold close in my heart and that I have seen come true over and over and over—with myself and others. As J-R has said, "The profoundness of the Traveler being with you is primarily that you're never alone." I've also heard him say that "you are awake in my heart, and your next step is to awaken to me in *your* heart."

Here's a note I got from a woman who had emailed a letter to J-R. She emailed back soon after she sent the first letter and told me, "You don't need to bother J-R with this now. I have gotten my own answers. I seemed to have to write him directly and then do s.e.'s to be able to get my answers." That seems to be a big key: reach out to the Traveler—inwardly, by writing and burning the letter, by writing and mailing the letter—and then open to the inner guidance.

And it can be quick. Here's a letter from a man who wrote that he had been feeling very low and depressed. He ran across a reminder to himself to write to J-R, and he said that "once I did start and had the 'Dear J-R' ready, things started to shift." He ended up not sending a letter about feeling depressed. To me, that speaks to the power of our intention to connect with the Traveler, which allows that loving support to start flooding in. Or maybe it floods out from within us.

One woman shared a wonderful story: "There was a forest fire coming towards our house, and the police told us we needed to be ready to evacuate. I called the MSIA office at 4:00AM and just left a brief message about this and asked for Light. As soon as I made that call, the wind changed direction, away from our house, and we didn't need to evacuate after all."

Coincidence? Maybe. But I don't think so. I've seen these sorts of things happen so often over the years that it seems much more than that. And when I remember that J-R has said, "I am always with you," I breathe it in and relax into that loving presence that makes life here so much easier.

Really Always with You

In the late eighties, I got a call from a person who asked me to let J-R know that a woman I'll call Susan had died about 30 seconds previously. I called J-R right away and said, "J-R, I have something to tell you." He said, "I know. Susan just died. I got her."

Some years later, I got a mid-morning call from a person who said that a woman I'll call Caroline had died 10 minutes previously. J-R tended to be a night owl, and remembering how he had known even before I told him physically that Susan had died, I didn't feel any pressure to call him immediately. So I waited until I heard his voice on the walkie-talkie about 10 or 15 minutes later. Then I called him on the walkie and said that Caroline had died "about 25 minutes ago."

He said thanks and then called me on the phone, asking when Caroline had died. I figured out the exact timing and said, "Seventeen minutes ago." He said, "That's what I have."

The day after one man in MSIA died, his wife asked if there was anything J-R could say about her husband that would support her. J-R's answer: "He has actually been here with me in Miami, doing spiritual work with people from South America. He is fine."

"Fine" seems a good place to end. I'm glad J-R remembers I am a Soul (fine) even when I'm going through my karma. I'll also be fine after I leave the physical body because I am a Soul, which never dies. And I am especially fine because J-R is with me through it all, forever.

So, as J-R says at the end of seminars, "Baruch bashan."

Glossary

Baruch bashan (bay-roosh' bay-shan'). Hebrew words meaning "the blessings already are." The blessings of Spirit exist in the here and now.

Beloved. The Soul, the God within.

causal initiation. See *initiation.*

chant. In MSIA, to chant Ani-Hu, Hu, or one's initiation tone. Hu is Sanskrit and is an ancient name of God, and Ani adds the quality of empathy.

Discourses. Soul Awareness Discourses are booklets that students in MSIA read monthly as their personal spiritual study.

Fulfilling Your Spiritual Promise. A 3-volume overview of John-Roger's vast teachings of Soul Transcendence. Includes explanations of broad concepts (e.g., karma, incarnation, and the human consciousness) and information about such areas as relationships, dreams, initiation, and his own spiritual journey. Available in hardcopy and e-book.

The Heartfelt Foundation. An organization dedicated to assisting people in need through the healing power of heartfelt service. Founded by John-Roger.

initiate. In MSIA, a person who has been connected to the Sound Current of God through initiation.

initiation. In MSIA, five initiations are given physically: astral (dealing with the imagination), causal (dealing with the emotions), mental (dealing with the mind), etheric (dealing with the unconscious), and Soul (who a person really is); initiation tones are given for each of these. There are also 27 levels of initiation above Soul, for which tones are not given.

initiation tone. In MSIA, spiritually charged words (names of God) given to an initiate in a Sound Current initiation.

inner Traveler. See *Mystical Traveler Consciousness.*

Insight II. Insight Seminars presents a series of seminars designed to help people become more aware of who they truly are. Insight I is The Awakening Heart, Insight II is The Opening Heart, and Insight III is Centering in the Heart. Founded by John-Roger.

Integrity Foundation. An organization that supported integrity and service. Founded by John-Roger.

karma. The law of cause and effect: as you sow, so shall you reap. The responsibility of each person for his or her actions.

Light. The energy of Spirit that pervades all realms of existence. Also refers to the Light of the Holy Spirit.

Light Study. Individual counselings that John-Roger did.

ministers. After studying in MSIA for two years, a person may apply for ordination, and many people studying in MSIA are also ministers.

Movement of Spiritual Inner Awareness (MSIA). An organization whose major focus is Soul Transcendence, which is becoming aware of oneself as a Soul and as one with God, not as a theory but as a living reality. John-Roger is the founder.

MSIA guidelines. Don't hurt yourself and don't hurt others. Take care of yourself so you can help take care of others. Use everything for your upliftment, growth, and learning.

MSIA Prayer List. A confidential list of names, where people can ask that the Light of the Holy Spirit be sent to a person, place, situation, animal, etc., for the highest good. Accessible online (http://www.msia.org/prayer) or by calling the MSIA office.

Mystical Traveler. Refers to the person or persons who are physically anchoring the energy of the Mystical Traveler Consciousness on the planet.

Mystical Traveler Consciousness. An energy from the highest source whose spiritual directive on Earth is awakening people to the awareness of the Soul. This consciousness exists within each person as the inner Traveler.

organizations John-Roger founded. Currently operational: Movement of Spiritual Inner Awareness (MSIA), Peace Theological Seminary & College of Philosophy (PTS), University of Santa Monica (USM), Insight Seminars, Institute for Individual and World Peace (IIWP), and The Heartfelt Foundation.

PAT IV. The fourth in a series of Peace Awareness Trainings. The PAT IV trips have been to Israel, Egypt, and Italy.

Prana. The building in Los Angeles that houses residents and the main MSIA office. Now more officially called Peace Awareness Labyrinth and Gardens.

seminar. A talk given by John-Roger or John Morton.

sister organizations. See *organizations John-Roger founded.*

Soul. The extension of God individualized within each human being. The divine in each person, the indwelling Christ, the God within.

Soul initiation. See *initiation.*

Soul realm. The first level where the Soul is consciously aware of its true nature, its pure beingness, its oneness with God.

Soul Transcendence. The process of moving the consciousness into the Soul realm and beyond.

Sound Current. The audible energy that flows from God through all realms. The spiritual energy on which a person returns to the heart of God.

Spirit. The essence of creation. Infinite and eternal.

tones. See *initiation tone.*

Traveler. See *Mystical Traveler* and *Mystical Traveler Consciousness.*

27 levels above Soul. See *initiation.*

Additional Resources and Study Materials by John-Roger, D.S.S.

Books

Fulfilling Your Spiritual Promise

If you ever had a question for John-Roger, chances are you'll find it answered here.

This 3-volume set of books is a compendium of information John-Roger has shared over many years. Along with an index that makes finding topics easy, its 24 chapters include a wealth of information on subjects including karma, the Mystical Traveler, initiation, and dreams, as well as attitude, relationships, health, and practical spirituality. And at just $45 for the whole hardbound set, this resource is a great buy.

Hardbound, 3-book set

ISBN: 978-1-893020-17-7, $45.00

e-book: ISBN: 978-1-893020-65-8, $25.00

The Wayshower

This book shows that John-Roger has indeed traveled the path to awakening. Not just this time around, but many times before. And he didn't always make the trip very successfully by some standards. Yet each excursion revealed to him more and more about the journey—one we are all on in our own way.

John-Roger has been many things, in this life and in others. So have we. The thing is, he remembers and has learned from them.

Here you will discover that all the things John-Roger has been have prepared him for what he is today: a Wayshower.

Softbound: ISBN: 978-1-935492-76-4, $8.95
e-book: ISBN: 978-1-935492-77-1, $7.20

When Are You Coming Home?
A Personal Guide to Soul Transcendence
(with Pauli Sanderson, D.S.S.)

An intimate account of spiritual awakening that contains the elements of an adventure story. How did John-Roger attain the awareness of who he truly is? He approached life like a scientist in a laboratory. He found methods for integrating the sacred with the mundane, the practical with the mystical. He noted what worked and what didn't.

Along with some fascinating stories, you will find in this book many practical keys for making your own life work better, for attuning to the source of wisdom that is always within you, and for making every day propel you further on your exciting adventure home.

Hardbound: ISBN: 978-1-893020-23-8, $19.95
e-book: ISBN: 978-1-893020-68-9, $11.25

Audio

The Wayshower

In this four-seminar CD packet, you can hear directly from John-Roger the stories of his spiritual journey that inspired the book of the same name. The seminars include: The Search for a Master, The Master and the Mudhole, My Kingdom for a Horse, and The True Self. The stories are funny and poignant, leading up to the profound message of the spiritual work John-Roger is here to do. Listening to J-R's personal stories of his quest is inspiring, whether you have been on a spiritual path for a while or are new to inner spiritual experiences.

4-CD packet: #3901-CD, $25

SOUL AWARENESS DISCOURSES
A COURSE IN SOUL TRANSCENDENCE

Soul Awareness Discourses are designed to teach Soul Transcendence, which is becoming aware of yourself as a Soul and as one with God, not as a theory, but as a living reality. They are for people who want a consistent, time-proven approach to their spiritual unfoldment.

A set of Soul Awareness Discourses consists of 12 booklets, one to study and contemplate each month of the year. As you read each Discourse, you can activate an awareness of your divine essence and deepen your relationship with God.

Spiritual in essence, Discourses are compatible with religious beliefs you might hold. In fact, most people find that Discourses support the experience of whatever path, philosophy, or religion (if any) they choose to follow. Simply put, Discourses are about eternal truths and the wisdom of the heart.

The first year of Discourses addresses topics ranging from creating success in the world to working hand-in-hand with Spirit.

A yearly set of Discourses is regularly $100. MSIA is offering the first year of Discourses at an introductory price of $50. Discourses come with a full, no-questions-asked, money-back guarantee. If at any time you decide this course of study is not right for you, simply return it, and you will promptly receive a full refund.

TO ORDER

To order John-Roger's books, Discourses, or audio and video materials, contact MSIA at 1-800-899-2665, order@msia.org, or simply visit the online store at www.msia.org

About the Authors

John-Roger, D.S.S.

A teacher and lecturer of international stature, John-Roger is an inspiration in the lives of many people around the world. For over five decades, his wisdom, humor, common sense, and love have helped people discover the Spirit within themselves and find health, peace, and prosperity.

With two co-authored books on the *New York Times* Bestseller List to his credit, and more than four dozen self-help books and audio albums, John-Roger offers extraordinary insights on a wide range of topics. He is the founder and spiritual adviser of the nondenominational Church of the Movement of Spiritual Inner Awareness (MSIA), which focuses on Soul Transcendence; founder, first president, and now chancellor of the University of

Santa Monica; founder and chancellor of Peace Theological Seminary & College of Philosophy; chancellor of Insight University; and founder and spiritual adviser of the Institute for Individual and World Peace and of The Heartfelt Foundation.

John-Roger has given over 6,000 lectures and seminars worldwide, many of which are televised nationally on his cable program, "That Which Is," through the Network of Wisdoms. He has appeared on numerous radio and television shows and has been a featured guest on "Larry King Live." He also co-wrote and co-produced the movies "Spiritual Warriors" and "The Wayshower."

An educator and minister by profession, John-Roger continues to transform lives by educating people in the wisdom of the spiritual heart.

Betsy Alexander

Betsy Alexander has studied with John-Roger for forty years. She joined the MSIA staff in 1984, where she has worked on books and other MSIA publications and assisted with letters to him and John Morton, She holds master's degrees from USM and PTS.

For more information about John-Roger, you may also visit:
www.john-roger.org

For author interviews & speaking engagements,
please contact Angel Harper:
Mandeville Press
3500 West Adams Blvd.
Los Angeles, CA 90018
323-737-4055 x 1180
angel@mandevillepress.org

MANDEVILLE PRESS

P.O. Box 513935
Los Angeles, CA 90051-1935
323-737-4055

www.mandevillepress.org
jrbooks@mandevillepress.org

www.ingramcontent.com/pod-product-compliance
Lightning Source LLC
La Vergne TN
LVHW051016080826
845145LV00009B/2661

* 9 7 8 1 9 3 6 5 1 4 7 1 7 *